Michael Chinery

Animals in the Zoo

Photographs by Michael Lyster

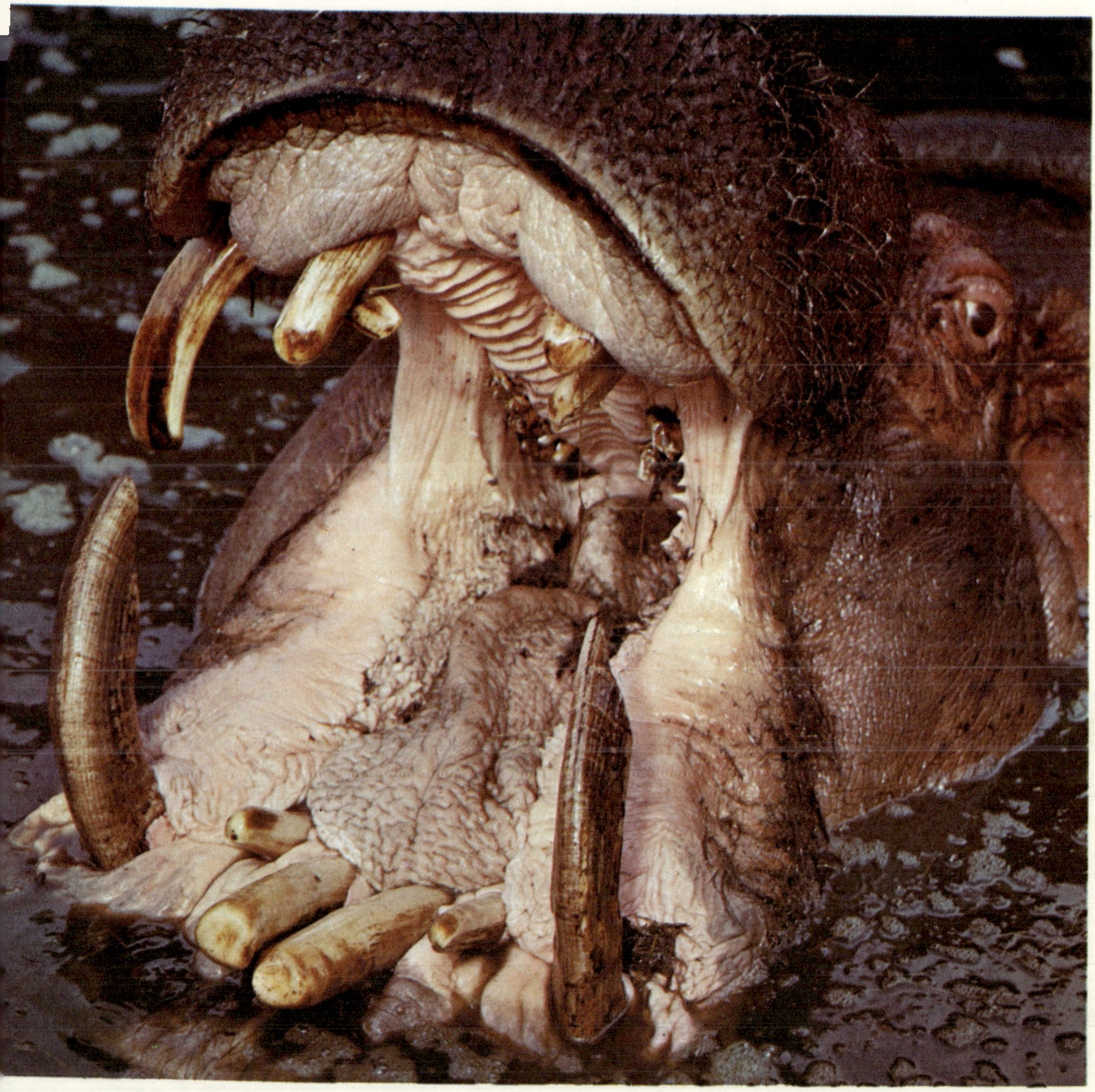

Taplinger Publishing Co., Inc., New York

Contents

First published in the United States in 1974 by Taplinger Publishing Co., Inc., New York, New York

ISBN 0 8008 0273 X
Library of Congress Catalog Card Number: 73-18792

Introduction

England's London Zoo and Whipsnade Park house two of the world's finest and most extensive wildlife collections. Specially prepared with the co-operation of the London Zoological Society, this book was designed to interest beginning naturalists on both sides of the Atlantic by presenting a superbly illustrated and wide-ranging overview of the lifestyle and habits of all major types of wildlife including large and small mammals, marsupials, birds, reptiles and insects.

The London Zoo, located in Regent's Park, was opened in 1828. The original site was much smaller than that occupied by the Zoo today, and the collection of animals was very much smaller and less varied than today's more than 1,400 species.

During the early years, nearly all of the animals were kept in small cages inside the buildings. It was thought that animals from warmer lands could not survive out of doors in the British climate. This is true of many reptiles and other cold-blooded animals, but certainly not of the larger mammals. Carl Hagenbeck showed how well they can adapt themselves to cooler climates when he started to house tropical mammals out of doors in Germany at the end of the 19th century.

London Zoo soon followed Hagenbeck's lead, and one of the most striking developments came in 1913 with the building of the Mappin Terraces—a miniature mountain where visitors can see sheep and goats climbing over a near-natural rocky terrain.

With an area of only thirty-six acres, London Zoo is small by today's standards. Nevertheless, it houses one of the most varied animal collections in the world. The emphasis is on exhibiting breeding groups of animals. This has meant a reduction in the number of species on show, but the Zoo still exhibits representatives of almost all of the major animal groups. In this respect it plays an important educational role. In addition, the breeding groups form more interesting exhibits than individual animals, and they make an important contribution to the conservation of wild species.

Whipsnade Park was opened in 1931. Although intended partly as a rest centre for the animals from Regent's Park, it soon became an important zoo in its own right. There are fewer species here than at the London Zoo, but the animals are kept in larger groups. With its wide open spaces, Whipsnade is an ideal setting for animals which live in large herds, and it is on these animals that the park concentrates. It is famed throughout the world for its herds of antelopes and deer, and, more recently, for its herd of white rhinos—one of the largest herds outside Africa.

There can be no doubt that the animals feel at home in the park, for Whipsnade's breeding record is very impressive. About eighty per cent of the mammals exhibited were actually born in the park, and many more young have been sent to other zoos. The breeding herds thus play a very important role in the conservation of the species. If zoos can breed their own animals, there will be no need to take specimens from the wild.

Large Mammals

Mammals are warm-blooded animals whose young feed on milk from their mother's body. They all have hair or fur, although this is not very obvious in some species. Many are intelligent and can be readily trained.

The largest land-living mammals are the elephants. There are two species—the African and the Indian or Asiatic. An adult male African elephant, the larger of the two species, weighs about five tons. Nearly all zoo elephants are females, for males are rather temperamental and can be very dangerous. Even the females can be dangerous. Elephants' enormous legs do not allow them to jump and they can be confined quite easily by a wide ditch.

Elephants are completely vegetarian and wild ones spend up to eighteen hours a day feeding on leaves and fruit. They often use their immense strength to push trees over to reach the upper branches. Elephants in the zoo are given more concentrated food and do not need so much. Nevertheless, a large elephant still eats about 100 pounds of hay and an awful lot

of fruit and vegetables every day. The diet of the elephants, and of all the other zoo animals, is carefully balanced to keep them healthy. This is why visitors are asked not to feed them. Too many buns and sandwiches are bad for the animals, just as they are bad for us.

The hoofed mammals or ungulates are grazing and browsing animals and they usually live in large herds. There are two main groups: the odd-toed ungulates, which include the horses and rhinos and the tapirs, and the even-toed ungulates, which include the cattle and deer and the pigs.

There are five living species of rhino and all are quite rare now. Three of them—the Indian, Sumatran and Javan rhinos—are in serious danger of extinction. The white rhinoceros of Africa was also in serious danger at one time. Conservationists have made a big effort to build up numbers on reserves, where they are protected. And now the white rhinos are flourishing happily.

1. *A living tank. The great Indian rhino's body is draped with huge folds of thick skin. Unlike the African rhinos, the Indian species has only one horn. This old lady keeps her horn short by rubbing it against the walls of her compound.* 2. *A grazing white rhino. Notice the wide snout, very different from the pointed lips of the black rhino, which is a browsing animal.* 3. *The elephant's trunk is formed from the nose and the upper lip. It is strong enough to pick up a tree trunk, but its tip is so sensitive that the animal can pick up a coin with it. The trunk is used mainly for picking up food and water, so hang on to your sandwiches—the elephants will snatch them if you give them the chance. They are also quite good pick-pockets!*

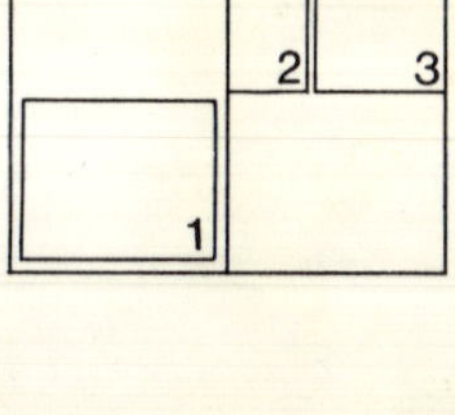

A breeding herd of about twenty white rhinos is thriving at Whipsnade Park, and it is hoped that this herd will be able to supply other zoos.

The white rhinoceros is not really any whiter than the black rhinoceros, which also lives in Africa. Its name comes from the Afrikaans word *wijd*, which means wide, and refers to its very broad lips.

Rhino horns are not true horns for they contain no bone. They are formed from bunches of hair-like fibres fixed firmly together.

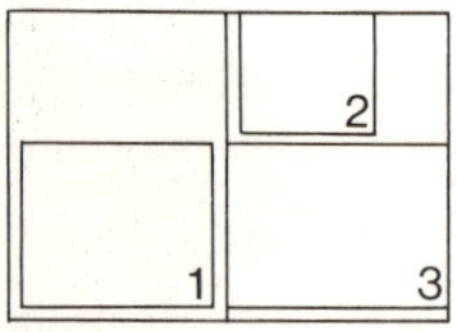

1. *The hippopotamus is an even-toed ungulate (hoofed mammal) related to the pigs. It lives in Africa and spends much of its time wallowing in the water with just its eyes, ears and nostrils above the surface. Notice how these are all on top of its head. The baby on the left is ten weeks old and weighs only a couple of hundred pounds. Adults can weigh about four tons.* 2. *The African elephant (left) is distinguished from the Indian elephant by its much larger ears, which reach well below the level of its eyes.* 3. *Two adult Indian elephants with a youngster, and a young African elephant on the left. Babies lose a lot of their hair when they get older.*

Horses and the closely related zebras and asses have only one functional toe on each foot. The only truly wild horse alive today is Przewalski's horse, a stocky brown creature found only in a small area in and around Mongolia. In the wild he is very rare, but survives well in captivity and many zoos have small herds.

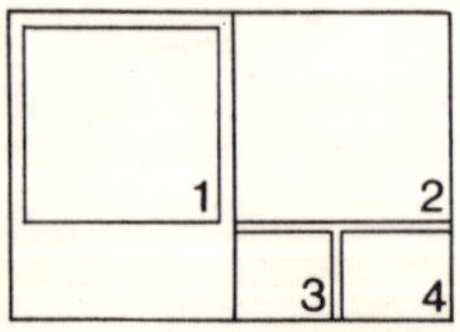

1. *Hartmann's mountain zebra from South West Africa. The mountain zebra differs from the common zebra in having a gridiron pattern of stripes on the rump.* 2. *A Bactrian camel. Notice its very broad feet which support it on soft sand.* 3. *Przewalski's wild horse showing the characteristic black mane.* 4. *Transformation: this scruffy-looking Arabian camel is losing its long winter coat to reveal its sleek and elegant summer dress.*

Even-toed ungulates include camels, giraffes, deer, antelopes, cattle, sheep, pigs and hippos. They all have either two or four toes on each foot. Many of them chew the cud.

There are two kinds of camels alive today—the one-humped Arabian camel and the two-humped Bactrian camel. The Arabian camel is probably extinct in the wild, but domesticated animals are widespread in north Africa and the middle east. A few wild Bactrian camels can still be seen in central Asia. Both species live in the deserts and they are well adapted for life in dry regions. The feet are very broad, helping the animals to walk on soft sand. The nostrils are covered with stiff hairs which keep out the sand. The animals can do without a drink for as much as two weeks but, contrary to popular opinion, they do not store water in their humps. The humps are stores of fat, which is used up gradually if the animal has to go without food.

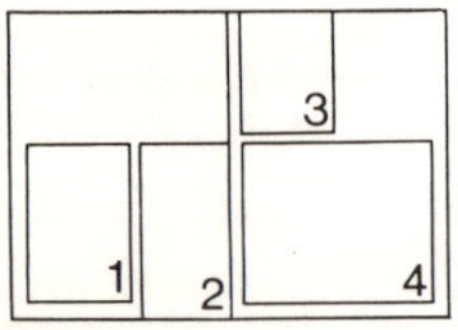

Four members of the camel family live in South America. They are the llama, alpaca, guanaco and the vicuna, humpless animals with long necks. They live on grassy plains and mountains. The guanaco is thought to be the ancestor of the domestic llama and alpaca. These two animals are widely used as beasts of burden in South America and the alpaca, looking like a heap of hair with legs, is also famous for its fine wool.

1. The sitatunga, a rarely seen swamp-dwelling antelope from Africa. He escapes from his enemies by submerging himself in the water, leaving just his nostrils above the surface. 2. Fallow deer in their winter coats. In the summer the animals usually become paler and their coats become spotted. 3. A family of guanacos, South American cousins of the camel. Despite its rather frail looking appearance, the youngster can run well, and has been able to do so from birth. This ability is very important to plains-dwelling animals which can escape their enemies only by running away. 4. Thompson's gazelle, one of the most abundant of east Africa's antelopes. The dark stripe on his side helps to break up his outline and provides camouflage.

The giraffe, which is found over a large area of central and east Africa, is the tallest of all the mammals. The males reach a height of eighteen feet and weigh as much as two tons. Giraffes browse on the leaves of various trees. They rip the leaves away with their lips and their enormously long tongues. There are several races of giraffe and each one has a different coat pattern. The brown blotches on their coats provide camouflage in the wild. Giraffes are timid animals and are likely to run away at the first hint of danger. They can cover the ground very quickly and often reach speeds of more than thirty miles an hour.

Deer and antelopes are very numerous animals and the two groups look rather alike. The most obvious difference is in the antlers or horns. Nearly all male deer have branched antlers which are bony outgrowths from the skull. They fall off each year, but a new set grows very rapidly. The new antlers are covered with skin at first, and they are then said to be in velvet. During the breeding season or rut, the males use their antlers when they fight one another for control of the females. Deer live mainly in forested regions and are found all over the world except in Africa and Australasia.

1. *Male and female blackbuck. Only the adult males develop the dark coat. The young are pale like the females.* 2. *The greater kudu, one of the largest of the African antelopes.* 3. *A young red deer with its antlers in velvet. The skin will soon peel away to reveal the naked bone.* 4. *Masai (left) and reticulated giraffes tower over the common zebra. The blotched coat camouflages the animals very well in their tree-dotted natural habitat.* 5. *Deer often cool off by standing in pools in hot weather. This is a very dark sika deer.* 6. *Père David's deer, with the forked front prong of his antlers, the long straight hind prong, his broad feet and long tail.*

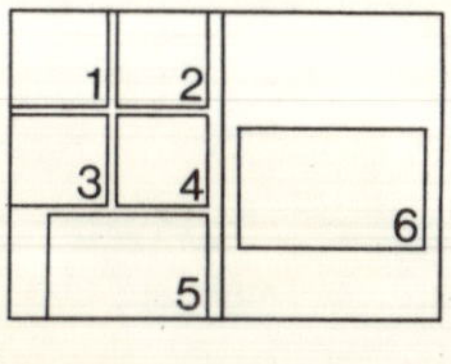

1. *Twin moose calves aged ten weeks. Largest of the deer, the moose (often called the elk in Europe) reaches a height of more than eight feet.* 2. *The spotted deer or chital is the commonest deer in India. It has a beautiful brown coat with white spots. Unlike most deer, the males and females live together throughout the year.* 3. *The gnu or wildebeeste is a large antelope which lives in vast herds in south and east Africa.* 4. *A female reindeer and her calf. Both sexes of reindeer have antlers, which is unusual. The female's are smaller than those of her mate. The spreading hooves help the animal to move over soft snow.*

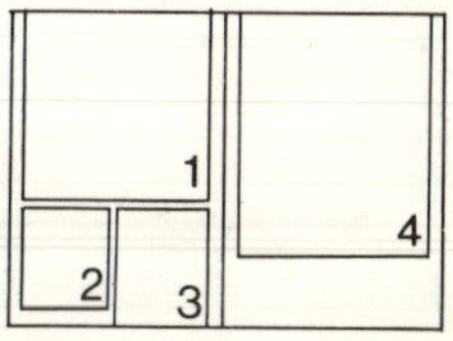

Antelopes belong to the cattle family. Their horns are never branched, though they may be spirally curved. The horns do not fall off like the deer's and they are made up of a bony core with a horn covering. Many female antelopes have horns, although they are often smaller than those of the males. Antelopes live only in Africa and Asia, most of them on the grassy plains. Deer and antelopes nearly all live in herds—large or small—ruled by a male or female.

The American bison, often called the buffalo, is a huge ox-like animal which can weigh more than 3,000 pounds. His hind quarters are relatively slender, but his shoulders are massive, made to look even bigger by the dense long hair round them. Bison once roamed in their millions on the plains of North America, but there was so much slaughter in the 19th century, that there were only about 500 animals left in 1890.

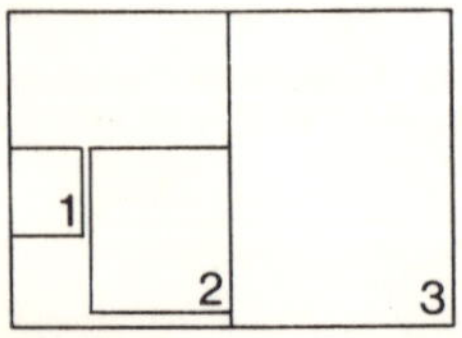

1. *American bison and calf. The adult's winter coat is beginning to fall showing the rich brown summer coat.* 2. *The European bison is more lightly built than his American cousin* (3).

The killing was stopped just in time and the animal was able to build up its numbers again. There are now about 50,000 living in nature reserves in various parts of North America.

The European bison, also known as the wisent, is the largest of the European mammals. It stands a little taller than its American cousin, but it is less heavily built. It is more of a forest animal than the American one, but it is extinct as a truly wild animal.

True buffaloes have long curved horns. Living in warmer climates, they do not have shaggy coats like the bison. The water buffalo of India and south east Asia has been domesticated, but the Cape buffalo has the reputation of being the most dangerous animal in Africa. Most animals, even

1. *Living high in the Himalayas, the yak is well protected by its long dark coat. Domestic yak are often paler in colour.* 2. *Barbary sheep from the mountains of north Africa.* 3. *The Cape buffalo, an aggressive and dangerous opponent.*

some of the big cats, will run away if suddenly disturbed, but not the Cape buffalo. He is more likely to send his 2,000-pound body hurtling straight at the source of the disturbance, flattening everything in his path.

The cattle family contains many hardy creatures, but none is hardier than the musk ox of northern Canada and Greenland. A dense woolly coat, with guard hairs reaching to the ground like curtains, protects the animal against all weathers. During severe blizzards, and when they are attacked by wolves, the adults form a circle with heads facing outwards. The young animals in the centre of the circle are completely protected.

1. *Sheep and goats are able to scrape a living from the rockiest hillsides. These Barbary sheep thrive well on the Mappin Terraces—the miniature mountain at the London Zoo.* 2. *A moulting musk ox. The thick under-coat which comes away each spring produces wool of very high quality.*

Bears are heavily built mammals belonging to the same order as the flesh-eating cats and dogs but, with the exception of the polar bear, they feed largely on fish and vegetable matter. Insects and small mammals make up the rest of the diet, and most bears are also very fond of honey. They

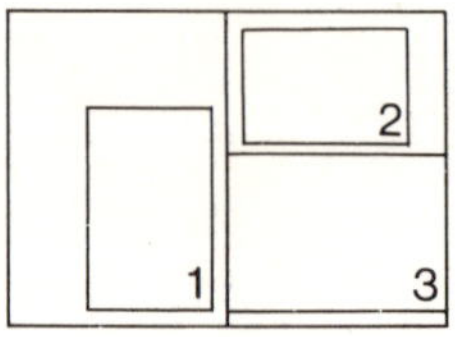

1. Bears are basically four-footed animals, but they like to sit up and often stand right up on their hind legs. 2. These brown bears are taking a great deal of interest in their visitors. 3. A female polar bear and her cub which is seven months old. Polar bears are very good swimmers and love to romp in the water.

often break open bees' nests to eat the honeycomb. Whereas most of the flesh-eaters walk only on their toes, the bears walk on the soles of their feet. As well as the polar bear, several kinds of brown bears and black bears live in Eurasia and in the Americas. They inhabit the large forests and the wild mountainous areas. Although not normally aggressive, these brown and black bears are not as friendly and cuddly as they might appear when they sit up and beg. They can be very dangerous if interfered with. A grizzly bear, one of the larger kinds of brown bear, has been known to kill a bison with a single swipe of his great paw. The sloth bear of India and Ceylon feeds mainly on termites.

Polar bears live in and around the Arctic Ocean. They keep mainly to the pack ice, and their broad hairy soles help them to keep a hold on the slippery surface. Sometimes weighing more than 1,000 pounds, the polar bears are among the largest of the bears. Babies are born in the winter, deep in a cave which the female digs out of the snow. Like all baby bears, they are very small when they are born, weighing under two pounds. Within a year they can weigh as much as 200 pounds and are ready to leave their mothers.

1. *A European brown bear—the original teddy bear perhaps, but not as cuddly as he looks. Notice his powerful claws.* 2. *Largest of the brown bears, the kodiak bear of Alaska. Notice how his weight is supported on the whole foot.* 3. *Probably the most dangerous animal in the zoo, the polar bear is a ruthless killer. He feeds mainly on seals, but is quite happy with other meat and fish which he is given in the zoo.*

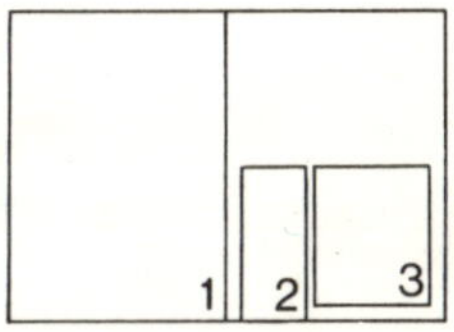

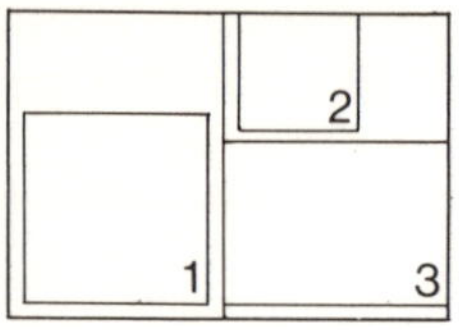

1. The wolf is a large member of the dog family and could well be mistaken for an Alsatian dog, although it is unlikely that domestic dogs are descended from wolves. The timber wolf seen here once roamed all over Eurasia and North America, but it is now found only in the wilder and more remote areas. Wolves live in small packs and hunt a variety of other animals, from mice to reindeer and even moose. 2. Although they come from the warm coasts of California, the sea lions are quite happy in a near freezing pool. They differ from the true seals in having ear flaps and also in being much more mobile on land. The sea lions can use their flippers to lope along, but the true seals can do little more than wriggle on land. 3. Feeding time at the sea lion pool always draws a big crowd of visitors, who enjoy watching the antics of these appealing creatures.

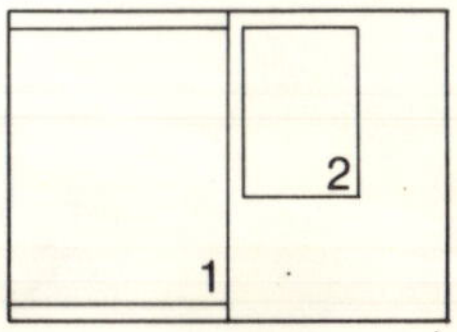

1. There can be little doubt that the most popular animal at the London Zoo in recent years was Chi-Chi, the giant panda. A member of the bear family, and distantly related to the red panda, the giant panda lives in the bamboo forests of the Szechwan Mountains in south west China. It feeds mainly on bamboo shoots, supplemented with a few mammals and fish, but very little else is known of its habits. Very few specimens have ever left their native land since the animal was first known to the Western world in 1869. *Chi-Chi was brought from China to the London Zoo in* 1958 *when she was at least one year old. She made headline news in the* 1960*s, when attempts were made to mate her with An-An, a male in the Moscow Zoo. In* 1966 *Chi-Chi was taken to Russia, and two years later An-An travelled to London. Both attempts were unsuccessful, however, and Chi-Chi, seen here with her staple diet of bamboo, died childless in* 1972. 2. *The red panda or lesser panda, a relative of the bears and the raccoons. It is a most attractive tree-living animal with a long bushy tail.*

The Big Cats

The cats form a very well defined family of carnivores, with their round heads, short snouts, and large forward-looking eyes. The snout usually has tufts of prominent whiskers. There are about thirty-five species of cats, ranging from the little domestic cat to the majestic tiger.

Strictly speaking, there are only five big cats—the lion, the tiger, the leopard, the jaguar and the snow leopard from the mountains of central Asia. These are separated from the so-called lesser cats not so much by their size—some of the lesser cats may be larger than the leopard—as by the fact that they can roar. None of the other thirty or so species is able to roar. Instead they utter a wide variety of screams and other sounds. For practical

purposes, however, the big cats are taken to include the puma, the cheetah and the various kinds of lynx.

The big cats attract plenty of visitors at the zoo, especially at feeding time. All cats are rather lazy unless they are actually hunting, and they spend a lot of time dozing in their enclosures. But as feeding time approaches they start to pace up and down expectantly. Do they smell the large juicy joints on their way from the kitchen? Does the gathering crowd of visitors tell them that food is coming? Or, do the animals have a sense of time that tells them when to get up? All three factors are probably involved.

The male lion, with his large shaggy mane, rivals the tiger in size. Both

1. and 2. *The lion is a rather lazy animal and leaves most of the work to the lioness.* 3. *A lioness keeps a watchful eye on her mischievous five-month-old cubs.* 4. *Chinese leopard cubs take a cautious look at the world.* 5. *The leopard is most active early in the morning and in the evening. In the middle of the day he likes to lie up in the shade of a tree or a rocky crevice.*

animals may weigh more than 500 pounds. Lions once lived all over Africa, the middle east, and parts of India. Today, however, they are found only in the southern half of Africa, and in a small part of north west India.

Lions live mainly in open savanna country, so their title "King of the Jungle" is not very accurate. Most cats like to be alone, but the lions live in small groups called prides. Each pride usually has a male and several females with their young. But there may be two or more males in a large pride of twenty or thirty animals. The lions feed mainly on zebras and various antelopes, and it is usually the lioness who does the hunting. Like most cats, she stalks slowly up on her quarry and then pounces, often breaking the animal's neck by her weight.

The leopard is the smallest of the true big cats, rarely weighing more than about 150 pounds. He is extremely strong, however, and often carries an antelope he has killed high into a tree to keep it safe from hyenas. Leopards are found all over Africa and the southern half of Asia, and they are the commonest of the big cats. Their numbers have, however, gone down greatly because of hunters eager to obtain their beautiful skins.

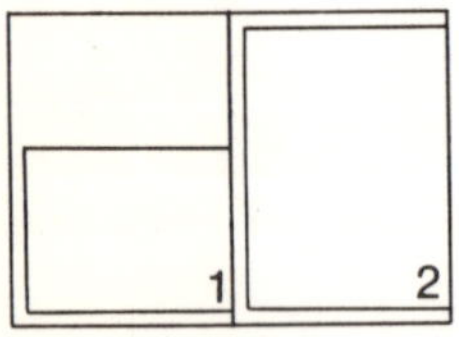

1. *Smaller than the lion and the tiger, the leopard is still a very powerful cat. Black varieties occur now and then, and they are called black panthers.*
2. *The puma or mountain lion, also known as the cougar, resembles a small lioness, but has a much darker coat.*

Largest of the big cats, the tiger is a truly magnificent animal, boldly marked and displaying a regal power and grace unmatched by any other creature. Most people associate the tiger with India, but he roams over a much wider area than that—from the cold wastes of northern China to Iran and the jungles of Indonesia. His original home was Siberia and it is only during the last few thousand years that he has invaded the tropical regions. Tigers living in these warmer parts are smaller than their northern cousins, allowing them to keep cool more easily. But they are still not perfectly adapted for tropical life and often spend the daytime cooling off in a swamp. If you want to see the zoo tigers at their best choose a cool day to visit them—even a temperate summer can be too hot for them.

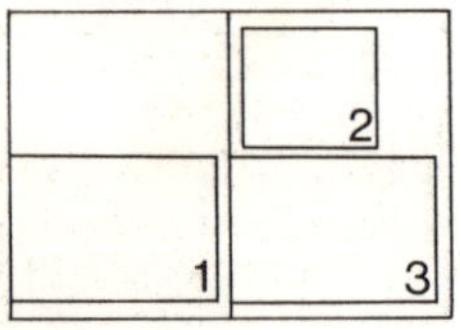

1. *Like most cats, the tiger approaches his prey very stealthily, his great paws making almost no sound as he stalks along.* 2. *At nine weeks the young cheetahs are losing their fluffiness. Playing with their mother helps them to develop the skills they will need for hunting in later life. Cheetahs have always been difficult to breed in zoos, and it was not until the 1950s that cubs were born in any zoo. To date twelve cheetah cubs have been born at Whipsnade Park.* 3. *Don't come any nearer! The tiger warns the photographer.*

1. The Sumatran tiger, smallest of the several races of tiger. Notice how the front legs are stretched out in front of the animal. This is characteristic of the big cats. The lesser cats, including your household pets, usually lie down with their front feet tucked up underneath them. 2. The heavily built and somewhat clumsy jaguar, distinguished from the leopard by the central spots within each black ring. 3. A proud mother keeps watch over her cubs. Like most young cats, lion cubs are spotted at first, but the spots disappear as the animals grow up. 4. Mother cheetah lies down quietly while her two fluffy cubs take morning milk. Cheetahs can always be distinguished from leopards by the black line running from each eye to the corner of the mouth.

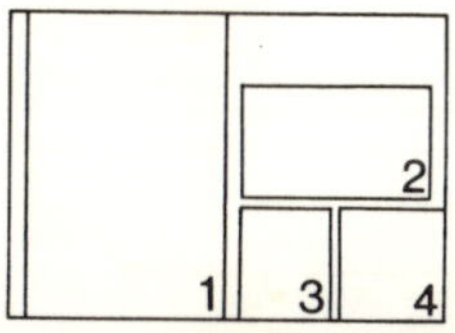

Wild tigers live in various habitats but they are most often found in the tall "grass jungle" that surrounds rivers and fills forest clearings. The bold stripes stand out very clearly on an isolated animal, but imagine the tiger padding through the tall grass at night: the stripes would camouflage him very well. Tigers feed on a wide variety of other animals, ranging from insects to the great water buffalo, but they seem to be rather scared of man, or else they don't consider him very tasty. Man-eating tigers do crop up from time to time but these are often old or injured animals which are perhaps too weak to catch larger or swifter prey.

The only true big cat in the Americas is the jaguar. He looks very much like a leopard, but you can easily distinguish him in the zoo by his stockier build and coat pattern. Living mainly in the forests of South and Central

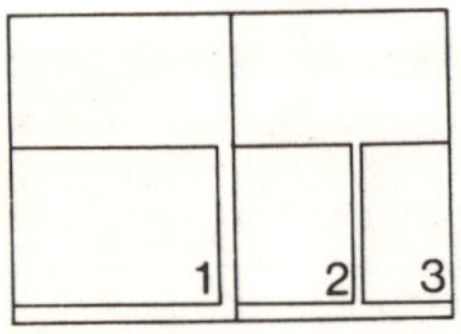

1. Bird-catcher extraordinary. The caracal or desert lynx can leap high into the air to pull down a bird. 2. The puma's snarl is largely bluff, for this is one of the more retiring cats and it hardly ever attacks man. 3. The northern lynx stares into space while waiting patiently for dinner. Lynxes can always be recognised by the tufts of hair on the ears.

America, the jaguar is sometimes said to be more cunning than the other big cats. He is said to run away from men and then to double back and attack them from behind. Actual attacks on man are rare, however, and it is unlikely that the jaguar is any more dangerous than the other big cats. He likes to spend a good deal of time fishing from a partly submerged log or an overhanging branch, cleverly using his twitching tail as a lure and then scooping the inquisitive fishes from the water with his paw. Various mammals make up the bulk of the jaguar's diet, but he is also fond of alligator meat and will occasionally plunge into the water to catch a fair sized alligator.

A third spotted cat sometimes seen in zoos is the cheetah, a supreme sprinter and the fastest animal on four legs. His whole body is built for speed, with long legs and permanently extended claws which give a firm grip on the ground. The cheetah can reach speeds of about 60 m.p.h. (96 km.p.h.) and he puts this ability to good use in chasing antelopes. High speeds can be maintained only for short distances, however, and the cheetah gives up the chase if he does not manage to pull down his quarry within about half a mile. Cheetahs are more easily tamed than the other large cats and they have long been used as hunting animals in parts of Africa and the Middle East.

Small Mammals

It is impossible to say just where the large mammals stop and the small mammals begin, but one criterion used at the London Zoo is weight. Mammals weighing less than about 35 pounds are regarded as small. These include most of the rodents or gnawing animals, many of the monkeys, lots of small carnivores and most of the lesser cats.

Most of the London Zoo's small mammals are housed in the Clore Pavilion, a modern building designed to cater for the needs of both animals and visitors. Many of these small mammals are nocturnal and, under normal conditions, they make poor exhibits because they are asleep for most of the day. The Clore Pavilion overcomes this problem, however, by housing the nocturnal species in the Moonlight World. During the daytime the lighting in this section of the building is subdued and resembles moonlight, and the lights are turned up at night.

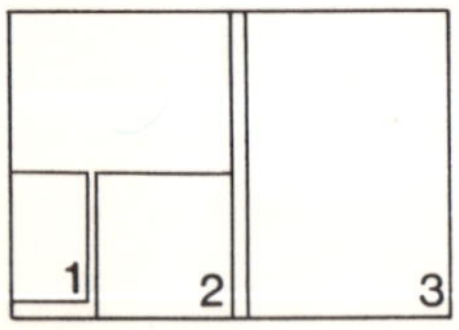

1. *The short-headed flying phalanger, also called the sugar glider, is one of Australia's pouched mammals or marsupials. It is active by night and makes enormous leaps from tree to tree, using its great bushy tail as a rudder.* 2. *The prairie marmot or prairie dog, a burrowing relative of the squirrels, loves to see what his neighbours are up to. He spends long periods sitting upright at the entrance to his burrow and watching the world go by.* 3. *The golden lion marmoset, one of the smallest of the South American monkeys.*

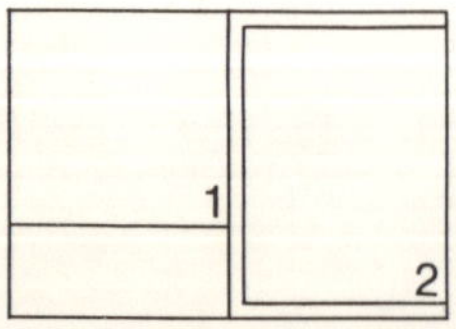

1. Posing for the camera, this blotched genet could be mistaken for a cat. He actually belongs to the mongoose family and is easily distinguished from the cats by his long snout and more slender build. This is especially noticeable when he moves about on his short legs. His long tail is held out more or less horizontally behind, balanced by his long neck stretched out at the front. Genet fur is, fortunately, useless to the fur trade. If it had any value these attractive African animals would be much less common than they are. 2. Tree-top gliders. The red-and-white flying squirrel is one of several "flying squirrels" found in southern Asia. They do not really fly, but leap from tree to tree, supported by large flaps of skin which extend from the sides of the body.

1. *One of the larger of the so-called lesser cats, the ocelot lives in the forests of South and Central America and reaches north to the southern borders of the United States. Its beautiful coat, patterned with a mixture of stripes and spots, is eagerly sought.* 2. *The fennec fox, smallest of all the foxes, lives in the deserts of Arabia and north Africa. It hunts by night, using its enormous ears to pick up the slightest rustle which might mean food—an insect, a reptile, or a small rodent. Hairy soles on its feet enable the fennec fox to get a good grip on loose sand.* 3. *One of the daintiest eaters in the animal kingdom, the crab-eating raccoon picks its food over very carefully with its front feet and very often "washes" it first by dipping it in water, even if the water is dirty.*

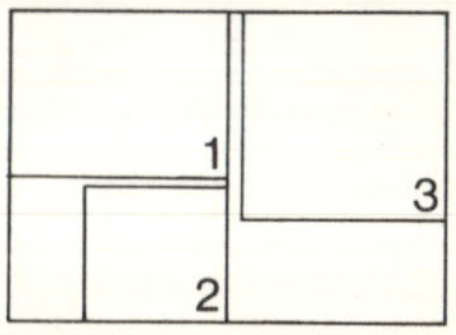

1. *Although only eight days old, these crested porcupines snuggling up to mother are already sporting a respectable growth of spines and they will soon be well able to defend themselves. The usual method of defence is to turn away from the enemy and then rush backwards, ramming him with the sharp quills.* 2. *The furry armadillo, one of the smaller members of this strange group of armoured mammals from South and Central America. Notice the powerful front feet with which the animal digs for worms and insects.* 3. *Gee up, Mum! This baby slender loris is getting a very slow ride, for Mum is one of the slowest animals on earth and each step may take half a minute. Special muscles in the feet enable the animal to maintain a vice-like grip on the branches among which it lives.*

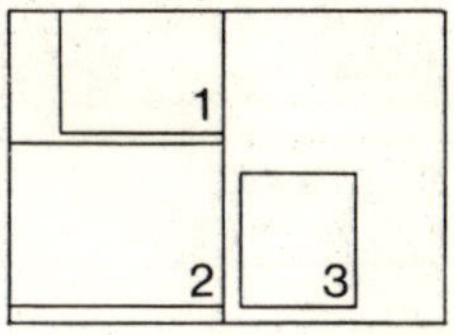

Overleaf: 1. *The ring-tailed lemur uses its extraordinary long tail as a signalling device. As well as having an obvious visual effect, the tail is used to brush scent on to rocks and vegetation or merely to flick scent into the air as the animal walks along.* 2. *The large eyes of the slender loris show it to be a nocturnal animal. It feeds on fruit, leaves, and insects.* 3. *This thick-tailed bushbaby lives in the thinly wooded parts of south and east Africa. It gets its name because it cries like a baby at night. Although related to the loris, it is a much more active animal and scampers easily through the branches.* 4. *The stone marten or beech marten—a member of the weasel family. Stone martens have become rare because they are hunted for their commercially valuable coat.*

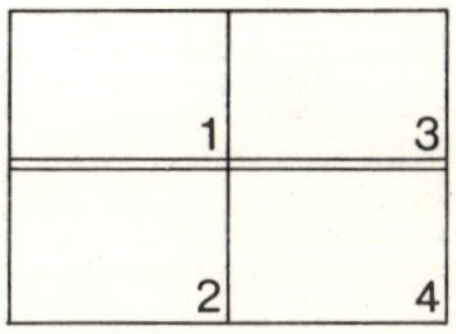

The only mammals that can really fly are the bats. Their wings consist of tough flaps of skin extending from the sides of the body and supported by the limbs, especially by the enormously long fingers. There are two major groups of bats—"big bats" and "little bats". The former live only in warm countries and their wings may span five feet (150 centimetres). Often called flying foxes, they are primarily fruit eaters. The "little bats" are mainly insect eaters, catching moths and flies as they flit to and fro at dusk. Their eyes are poor, but the bats have an excellent radar system and they can even avoid fine wires strung across a pitch black room. So don't worry about bats getting tangled up in your hair—they are far too clever. The zoo's vampire bats feed on cattle blood obtained from a slaughterhouse, and mixed with various minerals.

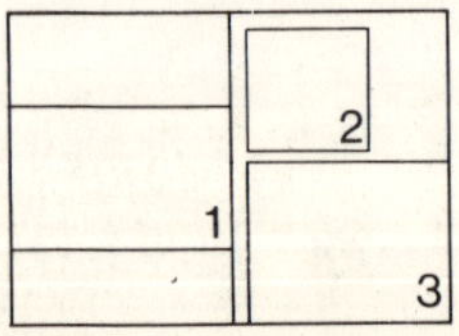

1. The elephant shrew is always poking his long nose into things. This is how he finds the snails and insects on which he feeds. 2. A large fruit bat or flying fox in its typical resting position. 3. Most famous—and most dangerous—of the bats are the little vampires. With razor-sharp teeth they pierce the skin of sleeping victims and lap up their blood without waking them. But the real danger lies in the bats' ability to carry rabies.

Apes and Monkeys

The apes and monkeys, together with a few other creatures such as the lemurs and bush-babies, form the group of mammals called primates. They are our closest relatives, for this is the group to which we ourselves belong. Most of the primates live in the trees and each limb normally has five fingers or toes adapted for grasping the branches. Life in the trees also calls for good eyesight and quick reactions, so it is not surprising that the primates have efficient forward-looking eyes and large brains.

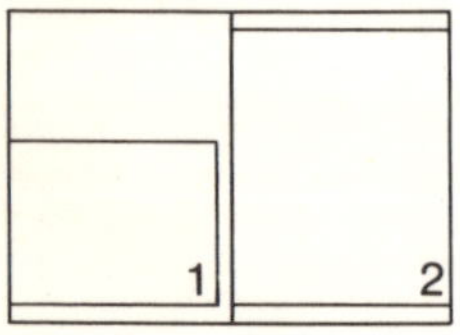

1. *One of nature's mysteries—the male mandrill. A forest-dwelling baboon from west Africa, he has a brightly coloured face and a rear end to match, but there is no acceptable explanation for his strange markings.*
2. *Popularly known as the "old man of the woods", the orang-utan is the second largest of the apes. His powerful arms swing him effortlessly through the branches or around his enclosure. The orang-utan is rare in the Indonesian forests now but breeds well in captivity.*

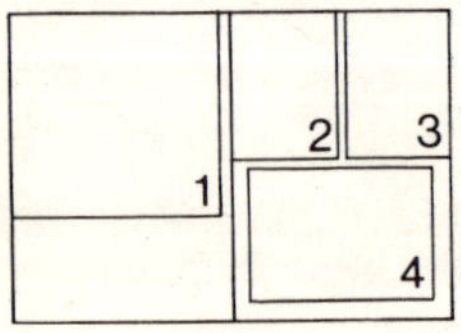

1. *Guy, the London Zoo's famous gorilla, in thoughtful mood. The silvery hair on his back shows that he is mature, and in the wild he would probably have been the boss of a small clan of gorillas.* 2. *A female grey gibbon cradles her four-month-old baby. The youngsters accompany their mothers everywhere to start with, clinging tightly to her fur as she swings easily through the branches.* 3. *A family of lar gibbons.* 4. *Lomie, Guy's wife, is much smaller than the male and, lacking the heavy crest, she looks more human. They have been together since October* 1971.

There are two distinct branches to the primates' family tree, one leading to the lemurs and the other leading to the monkeys and the apes. The monkeys themselves are also divided into two major groups—the flat-nosed monkeys of the New World and the narrow-nosed monkeys of the Old World. Many of the New World monkeys have long prehensile tails which they wrap around branches and use as extra arms. The group also contains the smallest of the monkeys—the marmosets, which differ from all other monkeys in having claws on their fingers instead of nails. The Old World monkeys, with nostrils closer together, never have prehensile tails. They include the colourful mandrill and many other large species.

The apes differ from the monkeys in having no tail. They also have relatively longer arms and better brains. They are among the most popular exhibits in the zoo because they are so like ourselves in many ways, notably in their ability to express their moods by various facial expressions. The only apes alive today are the orang-utan, the chimpanzees, the gorilla, and several species of gibbons. The chimpanzee is probably the most intelligent of them all. He is one of the few animals to use "tools" and he is very quick to solve simple problems.

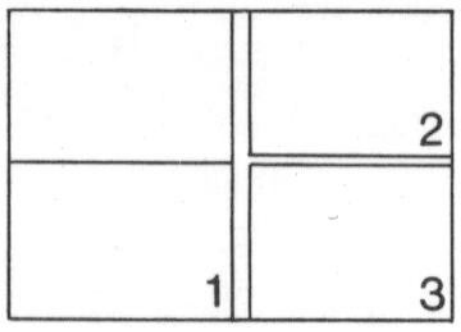

1. *Chimpanzees, which are probably our nearest relatives, breed well in the zoo and both young and old delight visitors with their antics.* 2. *Chimps are very intelligent too and they soon master an assortment of locks and catches.* 3. *The gibbons usually live in tightly knit family groups. These lar gibbons maintain their family unity even in the zoo.*

Marsupials

Kangaroos, wallabies, and koala bears all belong to a group of animals known as marsupials or pouched mammals. They are rather primitive mammals and the female cannot feed her babies inside her body after they are more than an inch long. The baby kangaroo is only about an inch long when it is born. It climbs up through its mother's fur to the pouch where it continues its development safely protected and feeding on milk.

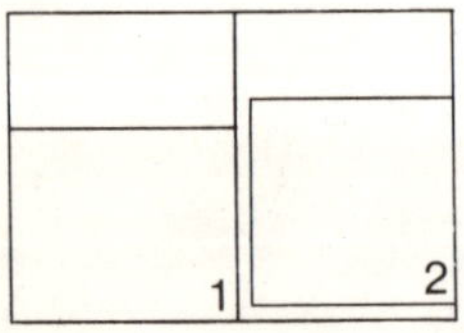

1. *Even when they are quite large the baby wallabies return to the pouch when alarmed. Wallabies roam freely over the grounds at Whipsnade Park.*
2. *Ever watchful, three Bennett's wallabies look at the camera. The opening of the pouch is clearly seen on the animal on the left.*

The marsupials have their headquarters in the Australasian region and the reason for this restricted distribution lies 100 million years back in the Earth's history. Marsupials developed in South America, possibly Antarctica and Australia before continental drift split them up. They have recently invaded North America and some of the East Indies. Meanwhile the placentals were evolving elsewhere and moved into South America from North America and towards Australia from Asia. Some marsupials became tree-dwellers, some became burrowers, some became meat-eaters, and some became grazing animals. The kangaroos and wallabies are the main grazing marsupials and they are the equivalents of the antelopes of Africa. Although their legs are very different, their heads are remarkably similar because they feed in the same way.

Birds

The birds, like the mammals, are warm-blooded animals, but they are easily distinguished from all other groups of animals by their feathers. These help to keep the birds warm and help them to fly. They are also responsible for the brilliant colours of many birds. The other most prominent feature of a bird is its horny beak.

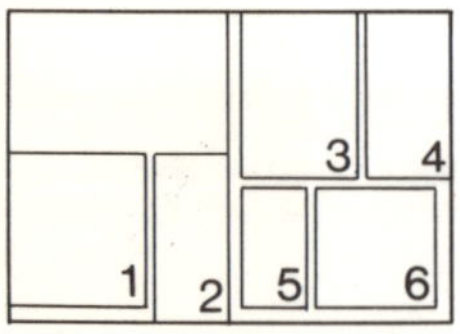

1. *London Zoo's Snowdon Aviary. Designed by Lord Snowdon, it incorporates a raised footpath that takes the visitor through the tree tops and allows him to meet the birds on their own level.* 2. *The rare perfect or yellow-headed lorikeet from the Lesser Sunda Islands.* 3. *With its beak almost as big as the rest of its body, you might think that the toco toucan would overbalance. The beak is very light, however, and the bird uses it very efficiently to pick fruit.* 4. *Yellow-streaked lory, another very colourful member of the parrot family.* 5. *Great Indian hornbill. It sounds more like a dog than a bird.* 6. *Cock-of-the-rock, a most unusual looking bird whose beak is almost concealed by a large crest of feathers.*

Among the most popular birds at the zoo are the penguins, which rival the sea lions in their ability to catch the fish from the keeper's bucket at feeding time. These quaint birds all come from the Southern Hemisphere, although only a few species actually live on the snowy wastes of the Antarctic continent. All are dressed in black and white, sometimes with red or yellow accessories, and they strut or waddle about like little men in morning suits that are just that little bit too tight. The penguins cannot fly, but few birds can match them when it comes to swimming under water.

---

1. *The sacred ibis attends to its eggs. Scenes like this are easily observed from the raised path in the Snowdon Aviary.* 2. *Saved from extinction the Hawaiian goose or néné almost followed the dodo but it was taken into captivity, notably at the Wildfowl Trust in Gloucestershire, and allowed to breed in safety. The scheme was so successful that birds have now been re-introduced to their natural home in Hawaii.* 3. *Two king penguins looking for all the world as if they are deep in discussion. Notice the large webbed feet, the long beak ideally suited for catching fish, and the dense scale-like plumage.*

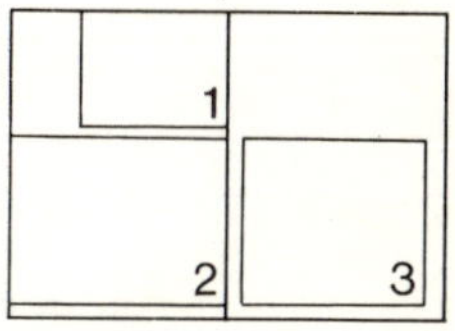

Their streamlined bodies are covered with smooth scale-like feathers and their wings have been transformed into powerful oar-like flippers. The wings propel the birds through the water as they search for fish.

Another very popular bird is the pelican, best known for the enormous "shopping bag" attached to its great beak. Although rather clumsy and even comical on land, the bird is very graceful as it floats smoothly across the water and it is an expert fisherman. When fishing the pouch is expanded and swept to and fro through the water. Several pelicans may combine for a fishing trip, driving shoals of fish into shallow water and then netting them with ease. Despite their great size—they weigh up to 25 pounds—the pelicans are also brilliant aeronauts, but those in the zoo are prevented from flying away by a simple little operation which removes the tip of one wing.

Many other attractive water birds live on the ponds scattered round the zoo, but the strangest are probably the flamingos. It seems odd that these beautiful pink birds should live and feed in the thick mud at the edges of a lake, but the spindly legs and the peculiar beak allow them to carry on without spoiling their plumage. The beak is sharply bent and can be swept through the muddy water without getting any of the feathers wet. The beak is fringed with bristles and strains small plants and animals from the water.

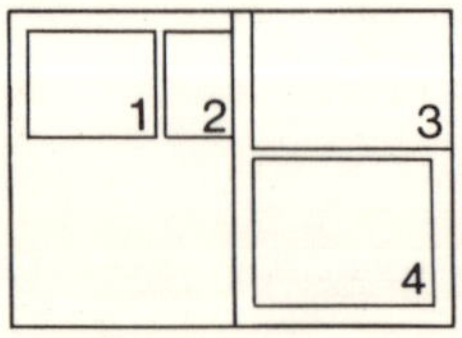

1. *King penguins searching for food in the water. Notice the narrow oar-like wings which propel the birds through the water. At other times the penguins swim with their heads up like ducks, although the king penguin does not often take to the water at the zoo. He spends long hours standing still* (2) *or waddling around the enclosure.* 3. *This somewhat comical pair of pelicans are using their enormous beaks to preen their feathers.* 4. *The very rare James' flamingo gets down to the seemingly revolting job of sifting food from the mud. He does this with the beak upside down.*

Among the ugliest of birds, the vultures are the dustmen of the bird world. They feed mainly on dead animals and they clear up what is left after the lions and other carnivores have had their fill. The birds have more or less naked heads and necks, allowing them to delve into a carcass without the problem of matted feathers. Their huge wings keep them aloft for hours with very little effort, and their keen eyesight enables them to spot dead or dying animals over a very wide area. 1. One of the largest flying birds, the condor is an American vulture. 2. Ruppell's vulture. 3. Watched by a Ruppell's vulture, a Griffon vulture builds an untidy nest of twigs. Vultures usually lay one egg and incubation is shared by both parents.

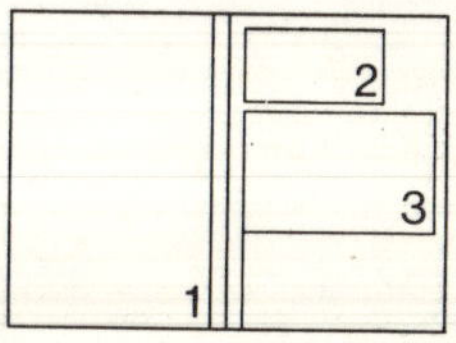

Literature is full of stories about huge birds which swoop down and carry people off to the mountains. Such tales are, of course, pure imagination. But if you take a look at some of the birds of prey you will soon see how such tales originated. The birds of prey are the meat-eating birds, whose food consists mainly of smaller birds and mammals. Some of them also eat reptiles and fishes. They are not all large birds but they are very strong, swooping down to spear their prey with sharp talons and then carrying it aloft on their powerful wings. A large eagle will have no difficulty in flying off with a young goat or deer in its talons, although most birds of prey take smaller animals. The birds always manage to look rather superior as they sit on their perches, the large eyes and the strongly hooked flesh-tearing beak giving the impression that they are "looking down their noses" at the visitors. They are not particularly active birds except when they are hunting and they spend lots of time just staring into space.

There are two major groups of birds of prey—the day-flying hawks and eagles, and the mainly night-flying owls. The first group also includes the secretary bird and the carrion-feeding vultures. Owls are beautifully adapted for night life, with particularly large eyes and very good ears.

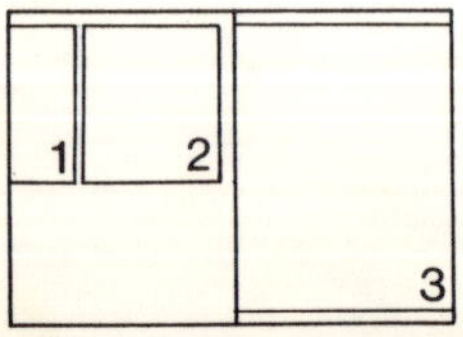

1. *King of the Birds, the magnificent golden eagle.* 2. *A pair of Javan fish owls.* 3. *The Chilean eagle feeds mainly on mammals, particularly rodents.*

Animals leading similar lives often resemble each other quite closely even though they may not be related. Nowhere is this more obvious than among the large flightless birds known as the ratites. The best known species is the ostrich, the world's largest living bird. Well adapted for life on the African grasslands, its long neck enables it to see enemies approaching and its long legs enable it to get away from them. Conditions on the Pampas of South America are very like those of the African grasslands and here we find the rhea, smaller than the ostrich but very similar. In like fashion, the Australian grasslands have produced the emu.

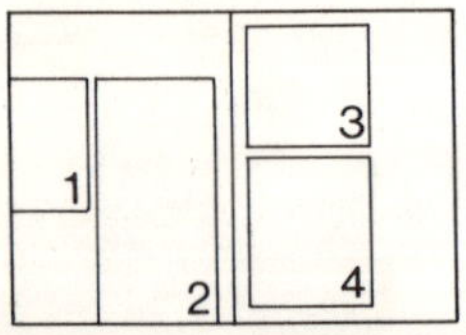

1. *The emu, the ostrich* (2) *and the rhea* (4) *all look much alike but they are not closely related. The similarities are due to the fact that the birds all lead similar lives.* 3. *The crowned crane from Africa.*

The pheasant family includes many colourful birds, some of them with finery rivalling that of the birds of paradise. As with most birds, it is the male who displays the most ornate and elaborate plumage, and there is good reason for this. The female does most of the incubation and it would not do for her to be too conspicuous while sitting on the nest. The males use their finery during their courtship displays, the most famous of which is performed by the peacock. When he meets a peahen, or anything else that takes his fancy, he erects his train to form a huge fan and stands there quivering. Many pheasants are now very rare in the wild and zoos are playing an important role in the conservation of these attractive birds.

---

1. *Pheasants breed well in captivity and many zoos have collections of these colourful birds. The golden pheasant, seen here, is one of the most striking of them all.* 2. *The secretary bird, so called because it seems to have lots of quill pens stuck behind its ear, is renowned as a snake-killer. It tramples the unfortunate serpents underfoot and then eats them.* 3. *Showing off! The male peacock is just as ready to display his finery to the photographer as to the peahen.* 4. *The imperial pheasant.* 5. *The kookaburra, a large Australian kingfisher, probably has more names than any other bird. Some are rude and some are complimentary, but the best known is the laughing jackass which refers to the bird's loud chuckling voice.*

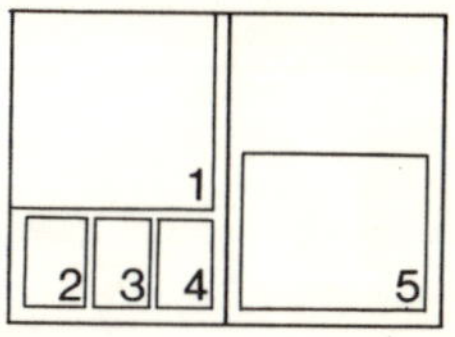

The noisiest place in the zoo is undoubtedly the parrot house, with dozens of birds saying "hello", "good-bye", and "pretty polly", and dozens more simply letting out ear-splitting screams. It is also one of the most colourful places, for these birds exhibit some of the most vivid colours in the whole of the animal kingdom. Parrots of one kind or another are found throughout the tropical regions and they vary from the little budgerigars to the huge macaws. But they can all be recognised by the hooked beak. This is extremely strong and it is used for cracking nuts, for defence, and as a third limb for climbing. The birds are famous for their ability to "talk", but they do not, of course, understand what they are saying. They merely imitate the various sounds that they hear.

1. *Better than any nutcracker, the macaw's beak can deal with the hardest Brazil nut—and it can get the kernel out without breaking it!* 2. *The African grey parrot, one of the best talkers in the business.* 3. *Distinguished from the other parrots by the long crest, the cockatoos are also among the noisiest of birds.*

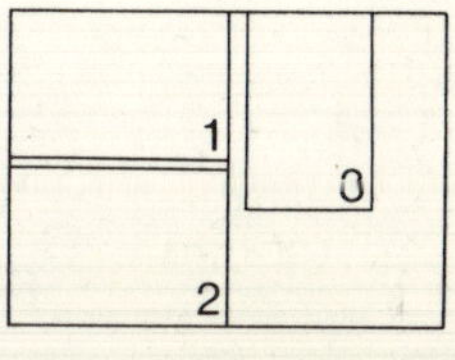

The brilliantly coloured humming birds all come from the New World. They include the smallest birds, some only two inches long and can be easily mistaken for moths as they dart about and hover at flowers. Their little wings beat so rapidly that they present a blur to the human eye and give out a distinct hum, hence the name humming bird. The slender beak—longer than the rest of the body in some species—contains an even longer tubular tongue which is used for sucking up nectar from the flowers. Little insects are also caught on the tongue's bristly tip. The zoo's humming birds are also given artificial nectar and they soon learn to stick their tongues into the little feeding bottles.

A variety of beaks are illustrated on page 61. Modern birds have no teeth and, with their front legs turned into wings, they have no hands either. The beak therefore has to do many jobs, including picking up and breaking food and building the nest. Look round the zoo and you will seen an enormous variety of beaks.

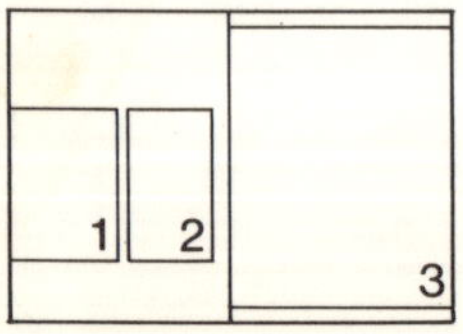

1. *Ponds serve two major functions in the animal enclosures at zoos all over the world. As well as providing drinking water for the large grazing mammals, they provide homes for many attractive water birds, such as this black swan and the mandarin duck* (3). 2. *This is the long-tailed humming bird.*

Reptiles

The reptiles are cold-blooded animals whose bodies are covered with horny scales. Contrary to common belief, they are in no way slimy and, although called cold-blooded creatures, they are not always cold. Being

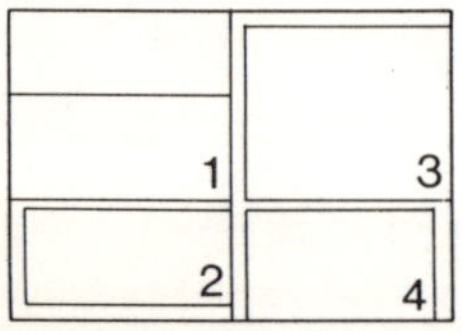

1. This toothy grin belongs to the gharial, a fish-eating crocodile from the rivers of northern India. 2. An obliging crocodile acts as a pillow for the gharial. 3. Slowly does it: a giant tortoise cautiously extends his head. Giant tortoises never hurry anywhere, but with a life expectancy of more than a century it does not matter. 4. The crocodile's upper jaw clearly shows the notch for the fourth tooth of the lower jaw. Alligators have no such notch.

cold-blooded simply means that the animals cannot keep their bodies at a high temperature in the way that we can. A reptile's body temperature depends on the temperature of the surroundings. On a warm day it will be high, and on a cool day it will be low. Because the animals cannot keep going when their temperature drops too low, the majority of reptiles are found in the warmer parts of the world, and this is why they are kept in heated cages in the Reptile House.

Entering the Reptile House and looking at the crocodiles, one can imagine oneself back in the dinosaur age. The crocodiles are the nearest living relatives of the great dinosaurs. They are rather lazy creatures and they spend much of their time just lying still, in or out of the water. They don't seem to mind being used as pillows by their neighbours, in fact they usually look as if they are smiling. But underneath that smile there is a wicked set of teeth, used in the wild to capture and dismember quite large animals.

Another very ancient group are the turtles and tortoises. Protected by their heavy shells, they have not needed to change much during their history and they look much the same now as they did 200 million years ago.

The snakes and lizards are much more modern reptiles, and these are the only groups with many living species. Several very poisonous snakes are on show at the zoo, as well as some of the large constricting species.

1. *Looking like some prehistoric monster, Jackson's chameleon sits patiently on a twig and waits for an insect to pass by.* 2. *Notice how the eyes and nostrils of the alligator are right on top of his snout. This allows him to see and breathe while floating just under the water surface.* 3. *Look what a big chap I am! The male anolis lizard inflates his throat sac to frighten an enemy or perhaps to attract a female.* 4. *The narrow snout of the gharial is an adaptation for fish-eating. He waves his snout to and fro through the water and the fish are trapped by the rows of long teeth.*

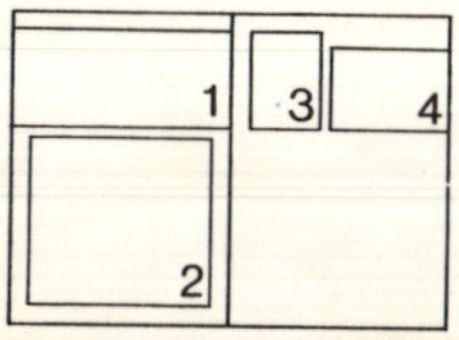

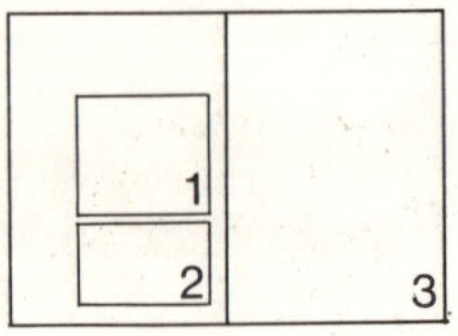

1. *Largest of the snakes, the anaconda or water boa exceeds thirty feet in length. Loosely hinged bones in the skull enable the snakes to get their jaws round animals much fatter than themselves. The anaconda will easily down a deer or a pig—and then spend the next few weeks digesting it.* 2. *Tree frogs abound in the warmer forests. Little suction pads on their toes enable them to grip the smoothest leaves. Frogs are amphibians and can be seen in the aquarium.* 3. *Camouflage expert, first rate fly-catcher and climber extraordinary: the chameleon is all three. Notice how his toes are arranged to give a powerful grip on the branches. He is famous for his ability to adapt his colouring to match his surroundings.*

Insects

London Zoo's Insect House was the first of its kind to be opened anywhere in the world. Here you can watch locusts, bred by the thousand to feed the zoo's many insect-eating animals. And you can see the inhabitants of a real ant nest going about their daily business. You can watch the praying mantis stalk its prey and, if you look carefully, make out the stick insects hiding among the branches. And if you wonder what goes on inside a bee hive, here is where you can see for yourself. But insects are not the only creatures on show in the Insect House. Several other groups of invertebrates—animals without backbones—can be found here, including large hairy bird-eating spiders and poisonous scorpions—all safely confined, it should be said, in glass cages!

1. *An animated gin trap. The praying mantis's head swivels to and fro as the insect works out the distance of his prey. His spiky front legs shoot out and there is no escape for any creature trapped in their vice-like grip.* 2. *Large numbers of locusts are reared in the Insect House to feed other animals in the zoo. If you watch them demolish a bunch of grass you will realise why they are such serious pests.* 3. *A Chinese oak silk moth, freshly emerged from its chrysalis in the Insect House.* 4. *If you visit warm countries, remember to shake your shoes and clothes before getting dressed in the morning: scorpions are about at night and shoes make good hiding places after a night's hunting. Not all scorpions are dangerous, and they will not usually attack unless provoked. But they will certainly give you a nasty sting if you put your foot on one. Scorpions feed on insects and other small animals, catching them with their large claw and using the sting only against awkward customers. The photographs show the jungle scorpion from India and,* 5, *the scrub scorpion from east Africa.*

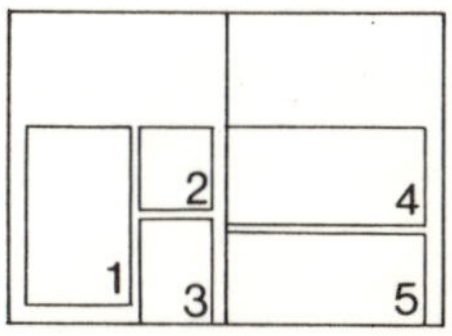

The Aquarium

London Zoo's Aquarium houses a wide variety of fishes and other aquatic creatures from both cold and tropical waters. Marine and freshwater animals are both well represented. As well as importing the animals, the

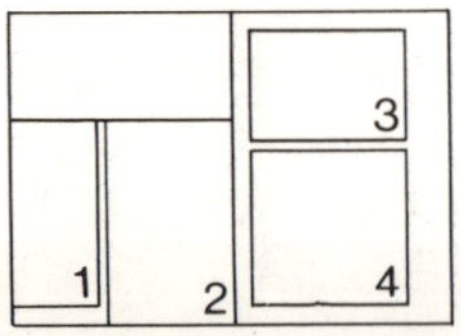

1. *Everything about the sea horse is unusual and it is difficult to believe that the animal is a fish at all. Perhaps the most peculiar thing is the way in which father is left holding the babies. The female lays her eggs directly into a pouch on the male's belly and he looks after them from then on, giving birth to the young fishes when the eggs hatch.* 2. *Much maligned, the octopus is generally a small creature only too ready to dart for cover if disturbed.* 3. *The piranha, a fierce flesh-eater from the rivers of Amazonia.* 4. *A living fossil, the African lungfish is a survivor from a very ancient group of animals.*

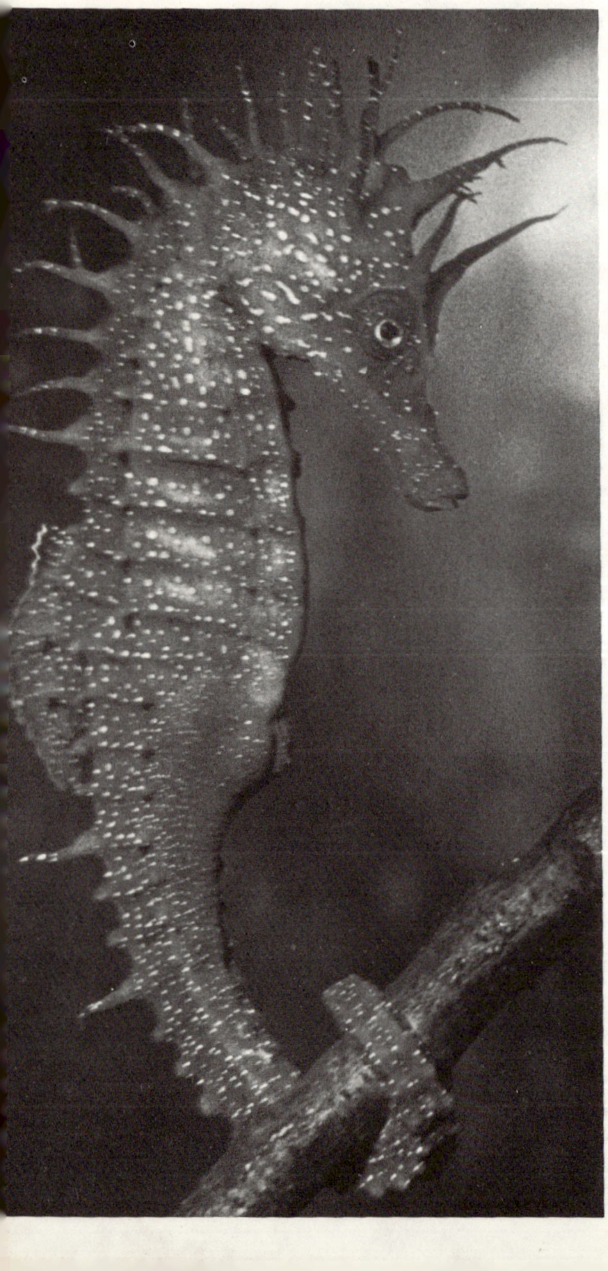

Zoo has to import the sea water in which to keep them. It is carried from the Bay of Biscay in ships' ballast tanks and about 140,000 gallons are circulating through the Aquarium at any one time.

Several rather primitive kinds of fishes are on show. Among the most interesting are the lungfishes. These have simple lungs as well as the usual gills and they can augment their oxygen supply by gulping air in through their mouth. This allows them to live in stagnant water and even to survive in the mud which is left when their pools dry up completely.

As well as the fishes, the Aquarium also houses the amphibians—the frogs and toads and the newts or salamanders. These animals have not completely abandoned the water and most of them pass through a tadpole stage as they grow up.

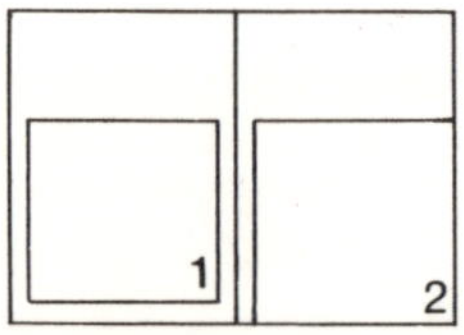

1. Colourful coral fish swim unharmed among the stinging tentacles of a sea anemone. 2. One of the major functions of the Children's Zoo is to allow young visitors to make contact with animals and perhaps to make friends with them.

Children's Zoo

The animals in the Children's Zoo are nearly all domestic. Many of them don't mind being stroked or cuddled, or turned this way and that to be photographed. In fact some of them seem to enjoy it—even following visitors around.

They are the kinds of animals you won't see in the main zoo and yet they are the best known of all animals, cows, sheep, pigs, rabbits. They have helped man for thousands of years but in this modern age many children who live in towns and cities never actually see a real live cow, for example.

In the Children's Zoo also there are some of the more popular pets such as Guinea pigs and rabbits.

Work in the Zoo

Man has been interested in animals for many thousands of years. It is not surprising, therefore, that zoos sprang up very early in the development of civilisation. Ancient Egypt, Ancient China and Ancient Greece all had animal collections, the earliest dating back some 5,000 years. The Greeks were the first to study animals scientifically. But with the decline of Greece, the study of zoology came to a near stop.

Zoology revived some 1500 years later when Columbus and other travellers were beginning to bring animals back from many parts of the world, and it was quite natural for people to want to keep these strange creatures and learn something about them. Many zoos came into existence during the 14th and 15th centuries. Most of them failed to survive, however, and the oldest still in operation is Schönbrunn Zoo in Austria. Opened in 1752, it still ranks among the world's foremost zoos.

Entertainment and Education

There are well over five hundred major zoos in the world. Among them they attract many millions of visitors every year. Most of the visitors probably go in search of entertainment—and they are not usually disappointed. But entertainment is not the prime function of the zoo. It is, rather, to allow and encourage the study of animals.

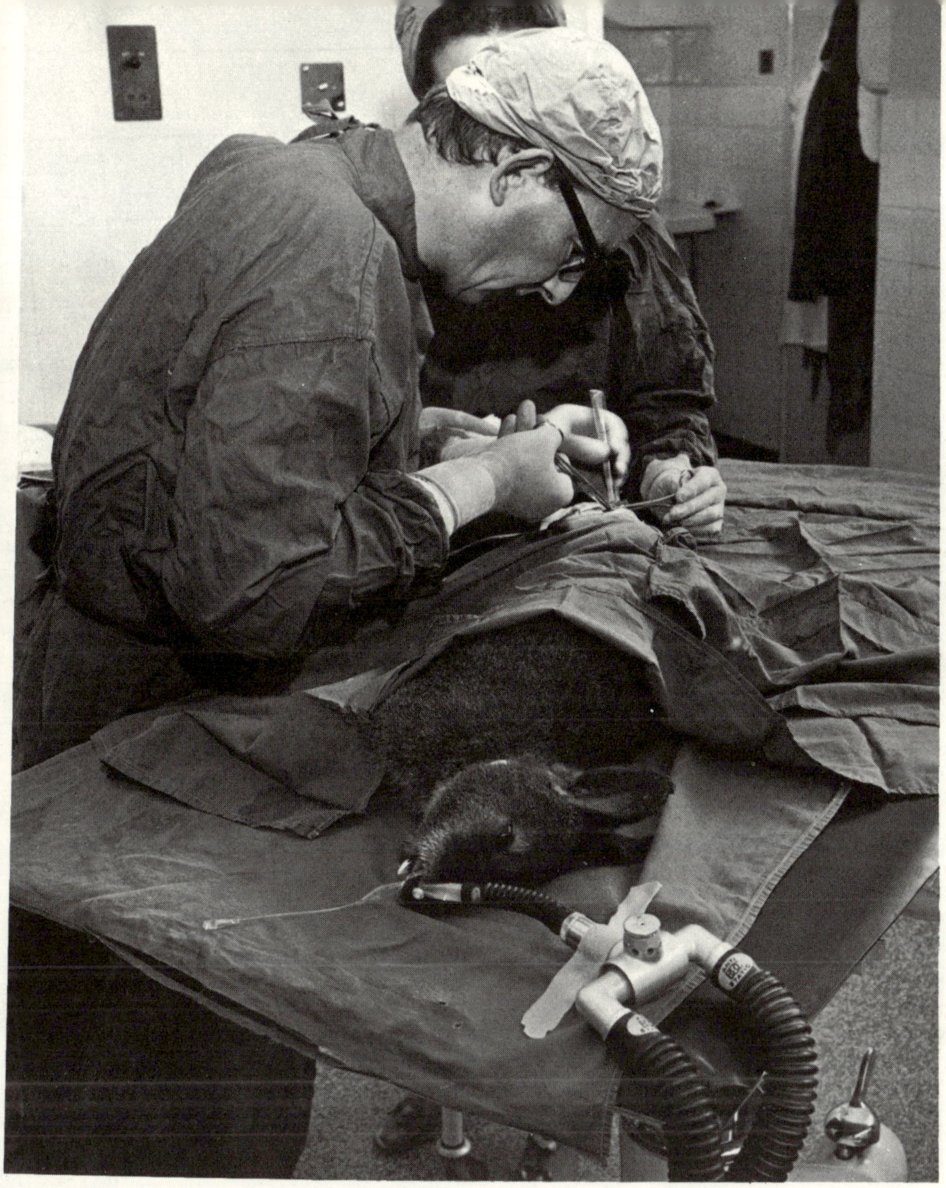

Only at a zoo can most of us ever hope to see anything like the full range of creatures in the animal kingdom. So zoos play an important part in basic zoological education. Many zoos organise lectures and guided tours and some have an Education Department which deals specifically with school programmes.

Zoos and Research

Learning goes on at all levels in the Zoo. Behind the scenes there is a great deal of research being carried out. The research is aimed at finding out what goes on inside the living animal. The London Zoo, for example, has two important research institutes attached to it—the Wellcome Institute for Comparative Physiology and the Nuffield Institute of Comparative Medicine. Much of the work concerns the reproductive behaviour of the animals, and the discoveries are frequently put into practice to encourage animals to breed more readily in captivity. More babies in the zoo is good for the zoo, and, as we shall see, good for the populations of the animals in the wild.

1. *A party of school children studying flamingos.* 2. *Operating on a sick wallaby.*

A good deal of research also goes into the nutritional needs of the animals —the types of foods that keep them fit and happy. Diet sheets are drawn up for the animals to ensure that they get the right materials and the right amount of vitamins and minerals. Many visitors admire the brilliant pink plumage of some of the flamingo species. This coloration is maintained in the wild because the food on which the birds feed contain a red pigment. Zoo flamingos do not always have access to these foods and, in order to maintain the birds' natural appearance, the scientists advised that an artificial pigment should be added to the birds' food.

Much research goes into veterinary medicine—the causes and cures of animal diseases. New arrivals at the Zoo are quarantined and screened to see if they are carrying any diseases, and all the parasites are recorded. Such information may be of great value in treating sick animals later in the Zoo's hospital. Another very useful research programme involves the building up of a library of animal X-ray photographs, again of great value in treating sick or injured animals.

All this research is obviously of value to the zoos themselves because it enables them to look after their charges better. But it has much wider applications. The knowledge gained can be used in improving breeding programmes for the farmer, in treating your pet dog, and even in improving the treatment of sick people.

Zoos and Conservation

The increasing human population of the world is demanding greater and greater areas of land for agriculture, housing and roads. So large tracts of

land are being cleared of their natural vegetation every year and the animal life is always being pushed back to more remote parts. In many cases the animals are in serious danger of extinction. This is well seen in Madagascar. Most of the island's unique collection of lemurs are in danger. Man has also endangered numerous species through indiscriminate hunting. Several hundred species are now in danger of extinction.

The protection and conservation of these animals is an urgent matter, and this is where the zoos can, and do, play an important role. If breeding stocks can be established in the zoos, the various species can be saved from extinction. And they can even, in some instances, be re-introduced to their native lands. The saving of the néné or Hawaiian goose has been mentioned earlier in the book. Another famous example is Père David's deer, a native of China and unknown in the western world until the 19th century. Only one small herd existed in China at that time and this was later wiped out. But some animals which had been taken to Europe were collected together by the then Duke of Bedford in order to build up a herd. Several hundred Père David's deer are now scattered throughout the zoos of the world.

A more recent example of conservation measures involves the beautiful Arabian oryx, a desert-living antelope often said to be the source of the unicorn legend. The animal was almost extinct in its native Arabia but a few survivors were rounded up and transported to the Phoenix Zoo in Arizona. Several young have been born.

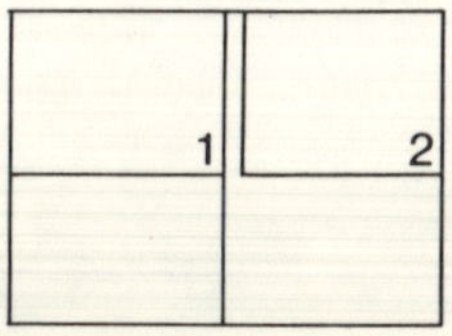

1. *White rhino.* 2. *Young ruffed lemur.*

If zoos can maintain breeding stocks of their animals, they can keep their own collections going indefinitely. They can also trade with each other: "We'll give you two young camels in exchange for your two spare leopard cubs." This sort of thing goes on a lot, as you can sometimes see by reading the labels on various cages and enclosures at the zoo. As well as helping the zoos, this practice makes an important contribution to the conservation of species. It obviously means that no animal then has to be taken from the wild.

There is also a good deal of co-operation when it comes to the breeding of rare animals. A zoo finding itself with a solitary specimen will make every effort to find a mate for it. This involves lending animals to, and borrowing them from other zoos. The most famous recent example of this was the attempt on two occasions to mate Chi-Chi, the London Zoo's female giant panda, with An-An, the male giant panda who lived in the Moscow Zoo until he died in October 1972. One of the most recent successes was the birth of a ruffed lemur at the London Zoo after its mother had been mated with a male borrowed from Paris.

Cheetah and Cubs.

Index

Page numbers in *italics* indicate illustrations